FACES AT THE MANGER

*An Advent-Christmas Sampler
of Poems, Prayers, and Meditations*

FACES
AT THE
MANGER

An Advent - Christmas
Sampler of Poems, Prayers,
and Meditations

J. BARRIE SHEPHERD

Westminster John Knox Press
LOUISVILLE • LONDON

Published by Westminster John Knox Press
Louisville, Kentucky

This book is printed on acid-free paper that meets the American
National Standards Institute Z39.48 standard. ♾

PRINTED IN THE UNITED STATES OF AMERICA

Library of Congress Cataloging-in-Publication Data is on file at the
Library of Congress, Washington, D.C.

ISBN 0-664-22808-9

I dedicate this book
to two "retiring" clergy colleagues–
honorary co-pastors of the
Swarthmore Presbyterian Church–
Rabbi Louis Kaplan
and Monsignor Frederick Stevenson
in gratitude for the grace and wisdom
revealed to me in their faithful ministries
and their genuine friendship.

Behold, how good and pleasant it is
when brothers dwell in unity!
(Psalm 133:1)

Also by J. Barrie Shepherd

Seeing with the Soul
    Daily Meditations on the Parables of Jesus in Luke

The Moveable Feast
    Selected Poems for the Christian Year and Beyond

A Pilgrim's Way
    Meditations for Lent and Easter

A Child Is Born
    Meditations for Advent and Christmas

Praying the Psalms
    Daily Meditations on Cherished Psalms

Prayers from the Mount
    Daily Meditations on the Sermon on the Mount

Encounters
    Poetic Meditations on the Old Testament

A Diary of Prayer
    Daily Meditations on the Parables of Jesus

Diary of Daily Prayer

CONTENTS

PREFACE

Two Christmases ago I had the great good fortune to discover that rarest of finds, a new favorite Christmas book. The text itself is hardly remarkable; it is the simple retelling of the Nativity story according to excerpts from the authorized King James Version of the Bible. The illustrations, however, make this little volume quite unforgettable. They are the work of an Australian artist, Julie Vivas, and they present scenes from that old familiar tale from a completely fresh, lively, and at times startlingly simple perspective.

One of Vivas's most intriguing and delight-inducing renderings shows the rough and tousled, plain peasant faces of four of the shepherds leaning over the edge of the manger, peering in gleeful amazement at the infant lying there below. The scene is painted almost from the viewpoint of the child, looking up and seeing these four homely visages, their jagged haircuts, bushy eyebrows, big noses, and rough hands, lined along the edge of the rude crib.

I guess this picture must have reminded me, on a subconscious level perhaps, of a scene from my own childhood when, at ten years old, I came home from school to welcome my newborn and first baby sister. She had been born on my father's birthday (just before midnight); and since, after two boys, he and my mother had been hoping for a "wee lassie," Heather Kaye was quite an event in our Shepherd household.

As soon as the bell rang for the end of classes Dick, my two years younger brother, and I rushed into the school washroom and scoured hands and faces; then we wet our normally unruly hair and plastered it down with the aid of a handy scrubbing brush. We were determined to make a good first impression on the new young lady. It was something of a letdown when, after the initial introductions, Mum told us that she could not really see us yet. After all, she might never appreciate the enormous sacrifice performed for her homecoming by two normally, healthily grubby boys.

The faces of those Bethlehem shepherds lined up along the manger edge and the memory of those other shining Shepherd faces from over forty years ago evoked in me this theme of "Faces at the Manger"—set me to wondering about all the faces that gathered round that straw-filled feeding box outside the inn of Bethlehem long centuries ago, and about all the faces that have been there in the centuries since. In poetry and prose now let us look around that manger and see with the creative eye of this holy, God-given gift—imagination—just who we can find and what they might be able to tell us.

FACES

What is it about faces,
tells us so much more about a person?
Hands, after all, are equally distinct,
each finger bearing signs which mark
the bearer as unique, unrepeatable.
Even the hairs of our heads
are not merely numbered, as Jesus
once assured, but by chemical analysis
can be made to reveal volumes about
the individual below.
Yet we read faces to discover
in an instant not only who a person is,
but how she feels, what he thinks,
and whether or not the attitude
displayed there momentarily
denotes affection or rejection.
Animals, fish, even insects too
have faces, highly concentrated areas
for gathering food, air, and information.
And at times we feel that we can see
emotion there as well,
the smiling of a dog,
the sophisticated boredom of a cat,
the panic of a startled hare.

What did he see, I wonder,
in the faces that confronted him?
Surely his sympathy,
his supreme compassion,

his ability to "feel with" those he met,
must have led him to great *in*sight,
to an almost miraculous ability
to *see into*, to perceive
what was going on within,
behind the visages
encountered on his daily round.
And understanding this, what a divine
forgiving patience to put up with
our attempts at dissimulation and deceit,
the foolish ways we try to mask
the truth of who and where
and why we are.

And as for his face,
why, the great galleries and museums
of the ages all are filled with our attempts
to reproduce those features that expressed
the true *Emmanuel*–God with us,
those lineaments in which we saw
for the first and fullest time
the grace of God lived out in gladness,
sorrow, and eternal tenderness.
Yet if we would believe his words
his face is to be sought and found
wherever hunger, hurt, and deprivation
are found within the family of God;
whenever love is moved to touch
and mend and heal.

I

AT THE MANGER

The little poem below in the traditional Japanese haiku form is an attempt to capture in miniature both the glory and the expectation of the Annunciation.

MARY'S MOMENT

Blue and gold align

Purity breathless awaits

In trembling stillness

*First appeared in *The Living Church*, April 3, 1988.

Some of the questions which must have troubled Mary's mind that holy night are explored in the two poems that follow.

MARY AT THE MANGER

And having come in, the angel said to her, "Rejoice, highly favored one, the Lord is with you; blessed are you among women!"

(Luke 1:28, NKJV)

Mary speaks:

Could it have been a dream, then, after all:
the towering angel, and the light so clear
and radiant, strikingly vivid,
yet so gentle at the selfsame time,
as if a flame could touch,
caress one's body even,
without pain or any burning?
It certainly seemed real at the time,
real in a way that nothing till that time
had ever been before.
I still recall the words I said,
or dreamt I said; "Behold the handmaid of the Lord,
be it unto me according to your word."
And so it has been,
for the most part until now—
according to his word.

The child that was foretold
began, indeed, to grow to life within me.
My husband-to-be, Joseph, somehow understood
despite the cruel and vindictive gossip—

told me of a dream he had known
of an angel bearing reassuring tidings
of the child that I was carrying,
the Son of God, the Savior.
And certainly old Elisabeth, my cousin,
just as the angel's prophecy had told it,
bore her son far out of season
and with all manner of rejoicing.

But this journey,
this journey in the bleakest
dead of winter, long and aching, bitter
with my tears and Joseph's fears along the way;
our welcome to this Bethlehem–
Joseph's ancestral town–
where the streets are crammed with soldiers
and with beggars, and the inns are full
and every door locked tight
against the stranger;
is this a greeting for the Son of God?
Is this the kind of blessing that was promised
when the angel called me, "Blessed among women"?
Such blessing may be better done without,
that brings me to this drafty cattle cave,
this unassisted birth among the straw,
this broken manger bearing so much hope–
both human and divine–
within its worn and battered walls.
"Blessed among women," indeed!
What kind of blessing did he have in mind?

There is a blessing, to be sure,
come forth from all that awkward pain
and sweat and blood last night.
This boy, my boy,
whose cry aroused the midnight,
whose sturdy frame lies nestled warm

within his bindings at my side,
whose hungry mouth seeks out my breast;
this child is surely blessing
beyond any I had hoped.
Maybe this was what the angel–
if he really came–was speaking of.
But does not each and every mother
know at least this much of joy
before the pain sets in again?
No, there should be something more;
something grand, I should say majestic,
to justify those special signs,
to bear this holy guarantee of blessedness.

Perhaps–perish the thought that never
crossed my mind till now–perhaps the plan
went wrong somewhere along the way.
Maybe the Roman census threw things off,
and if the birth had been in Nazareth–
as I planned it all along–
things would have gone just fine.
But surely God, in sending the Messiah
to his people, cannot be frustrated
by Caesars or by Herods and their schemes.
Surely God can cause to move
even the stars within their courses
to bear witness to his purposes,
to overrule the evil counsels
and maneuvers of such men.

Then could it be
that I have been to blame?
Have I failed in some requirement;
misheard, maybe, the mighty angel's message
in one minutely detailed point
and thus forfeited the blessing,
not only for myself, but for my child?

Please God, do not let that be so.
Did Joseph err, this kindest of all men
throughout these nine long months of
care and preparation mixed with
public scorn and rude humiliation?
Surely it was not my Joseph's blame.
And yet, the question troubles me.
What happened to the blessing,
that rich, mysterious benediction
that was to have been ours?

Still, here he lies at rest.
And something tells me that the blessing
which I seek lies deep in him.
Yes, within this tiny, vulnerable frame
there is a life which, like no other,
will bring joy to me,
to this whole world before its end.
Just look at me now!
A new mother this same day,
and already I am thinking of the end!
Still, there was a shadow fell
across my heart just now;
a shadow that reminded me
that blessing for our people
has never been what it appeared
at first to be.

To be blessed,
chosen by the Lord,
has meant for us, the Jews,
the centuries-long and steady pain
of exile, of banishment, of subjugation,
homelessness, injustice, and the lash.
We have born it like a cross,
this blessing God has laid upon us.
Yet out of it has come the law,

the prophets, and the wisdom of our faith.
Might it be this sort of blessing
that the angel had in mind,
a two-edged sword that has to cut
in order to set free,
that can bring forth sheerest joy,
but only when the price of deadly pain
has all been paid?

I suppose that, in one sense,
I have just learned this in my own life,
in my own body bringing forth this child,
this lively gift of God;
learned that blessing also
bears a wounding deep within,
that the granting of God's favor
takes away, at least for now,
the passing favors of this world.
Who knows?
For see, the babe
is stirring once again;
and I think I hear the tread
of footsteps coming toward the cave,
the bleat of sheep, as Joseph moves
across to guard the door.

Whoever's there,
whatever blessing is,
or is to be for me,
I feel this day secure,
secure as never in my life,
secure beyond all reason
in this cold and darkened place,
this wintered season of the world.
Secure because beside me,
yes, within my very being,
God is present, God is with me,

God is sharing in and bearing
through my child the passing laughter
and the tears that we call life.
God is giving himself to us
in this child he gives to me;
and if this grace, this purity,
this innocence, this love
I hold right now is God,
then I know blessing far beyond
any fear, any hope, any dream
I might have dreamed.
Don't ask me to explain.
Just kneel, my friend,
beside these shepherds.
Worship him in silence
and be blessed.

MARY:
ANNO DOMINI

What birthright does he bring
this bright and blood-born king
who rests within my arm
so body-warm and newly
fully living, makes me sing despite
a knifing weariness and pain?

His reign may move
the main a little, slow the steeply
spreading stain, may even
prove the deep and shining vein
of plain and honest truth
in talk and trade.

But laid across my body
burns a blade. His truth
must cut this bitter-braided cord
of breath and bone, set them apart
until, the debt of lies repaid,
he can, with royal dancing, bring us home.

*First appeared in *Anglican Theological Review*, Vol. 58, No. 4, October 1976, page 481. Used by permission.

Not only human faces gathered round that cattle crib. This poem looks at some other, quite contrasting, possibilities.

ANGELS AND ANIMALS

The creation waits with eager longing . . . because the creation itself will be set free from its bondage to decay and obtain the glorious liberty of the children of God.

(Romans 8:19, 21)

The mystery and the manure of Christmas.
What kind of theme is that for a decent, upright,
respectable Presbyterian poet to address,
especially in this clean and tinsel-shiny,
balsam-scented season of the year?
The mystery and the manure of Christmas?

Yet this unlikely combination
is precisely what we are faced with
when we recognize that there has been,
according to the evidence of scripture
and tradition, a place reserved
both for angels and for animals
within that holiest of moments
when the Divine entered,
became a living, breathing part
of its own creation.
The mystery and the manure of Christmas.

This confrontation comes,
although it shouldn't,
as something of a shock to us today.
We inhabit an increasingly anthropocentric world;

a society and intellectual mindset which has moved,
in little more than two centuries,
from Alexander Pope's historic dictum:

> Know then thyself, presume not God to scan;
> The proper study of mankind is man.

all the way to the current scene
where, indeed, "man is the measure of all things"
and all things revolve around,
serve the needs of,
and exist for the sake of,
humankind.

Even a century–
half a century ago,
people were in closer daily touch
with the other created orders of being.
Cows had to be milked, by hand, each day.
Horses needed to be groomed, fed, cared for.
Eggs were to be gathered,
barns, pig sties to be swept and shoveled out,
furnished with clean, sweet-smelling straw.

Once, in my early teens,
I undertook the herculean task
of cleaning–single handed–
a vast, Augean chicken house
at the rear of a local hotel.
It was part of "Bob-A-Job Week"–
a Boy Scout money-raising effort
("Bob" meaning, in our British slang,
one shilling, about fifty cents).
That was one of the hottest weeks on record,
and also one of the toughest,
most pungent "Bobs" I ever earned.
But I certainly learned a lot
about reality–chicken house style!

Most people today, on the other hand,
spend almost all their living hours
within a synthetic, manmade cocoon,
far removed from such natural, earthy realities.
We dress ourselves in manufactured fibers,
feed ourselves, increasingly,
with laboratory-devised nutrients;
we dwell in homes, live with furniture
created from synthetic substances,
and breathe in air which has been,
first grossly polluted,
then filtered, heated, or cooled
by humanly-devised mechanisms.
We move from one cocoon to another
by means of ingenious traveling devices.
We even entertain and inspire ourselves,
not with the sights and sounds of nature–
those radiant, austere winter sunsets
of this chill December solstice–
but with distorted images of our own devising
on a glass and plastic box.

We seem surprised,
almost resentful nowadays,
when such antique realities as snow,
sleet and hail, floods, drought,
earthquakes, volcanoes, and the like,
presume to break in, disorder, and disrupt
this tightly organized little world
we have built up around ourselves.

So it is
that when we look back
at the stories of Christmas;
when we are faced, for example,
with the fact that Isaiah foresaw

the blissful heavenly kingdom basically
in terms of peace among the animals:

> The wolf with the lamb . . .
> the calf with the lion . . .

and so forth;
or when we come upon
this record that Christ came,
not into a human habitation,
but to a stable;
and that his birth was heralded,
not by any pre-Christmas media blitz,
but by a bunch of herald angels
out on a lonely hillside;
we are not at all sure
what to make of it.

Are these simply relics,
leftover fossils,
the last traces of an earlier,
much more primitive view of things
when animals and heavenly beings
were accepted as a normal part
of everyday experience?
Or might there be a message here,
a word that calls out toward us
in our cozy, twentieth-century cocoons?

First, what about those animals?
It's really quite amusing
what we do with them, these creatures,
in our Christmas cards and sentimental verse.
We turn them into humans, for the most part.
There is no way we can deal with them
simply as animals, *per se*, and so
we dress them up into "The Lowly Beasts,"
depicting ox and ass kneeling at the stall

in absurdly awkward reverence.
Or we devise ridiculous TV cartoons
about "The Night the Animals Talked"
or "The Raccoons' Christmas";
quite forgetting that cuteness
had no part at all in the original
manger scene at Bethlehem.

Even our Christmas songs
warble, all too often, about
the patient ox, the humble ass.

> The sweet breath of the kine
> on the chill December breeze.

Have these people ever been in a real stable?
Have they ever walked, or attempted to walk,
across the floor of a humble peasant cowshed?

Several Augusts ago now
our family attended a wedding in Vermont.
After the church service
we drove out to the family farm
and feasted there on homegrown,
home-butchered, home-cooked,
fresh roast beef and lamb.
During a pause in the festivities
I took Catriona–my youngest daughter–
(who had never seen a cow close-up before)
round to the sheds for milking time.
The smell was almost enough, and the footing,
but we were finally driven out by the flies
that landed everywhere in vast
buzzing, swarming clouds.
Strange, but I've never heard
a Christmas carol sung about the flies
that buzzed in Joseph's ear;
the mire, the noise, the pests,

the stench that are a basic part
of the real world of animals.

To be completely accurate,
ours is not the first generation
to be offended by the stark reality
of that Bethlehem cowshed.
Way back in 1635,
the fastidious Queen Anne of Austria
instructed her royal architect
concerning one of her building projects
in these terms:

> The church must be a sumptuous and mag-
> nificent sanctuary, in order to compensate as
> much as possible for the extreme vulgarity
> and poverty of the place where the Eternal
> Word chose to be born.

How tasteless of the Eternal Word!
Now if only her majesty had been in charge.

Yet that is where it all took place.
Not in some pseudo-rustic, plastic stable
floodlit on the lawn outside the church;
nor in some over-ornate baroque
or rococo ecclesiastical excess;
but in the grunge and grime, the smell
and din of an honest-to-goodness,
honest to Godness, cowshed
somewhere in the hills of Palestine.

And it's important, may even be crucial,
that it happened there among the animals
because it sets us in our rightful place;
not at the center, where we like to be,
expect to be; but as one
with all the rest of God's creation,

animal, vegetable, mineral–
yes, the very stars on high
present and witnessing the birth of God
into the heart of his own creation.

Think of it–
the heart of this vast universe
somehow, some way, contained within
the wildly-beating heart of a newborn babe.
I am suggesting, don't you see,
that the animals belonged there
every bit as much as you and I.
I wrote a poem on this theme
some years ago,
called, "The Silent Seers":

> Of all the witnesses
> around that holy manger
> perhaps it was the animals
> saw best what lay ahead
> for they had paced the aching roads
> slept in the wet and hungry fields
> known the sharp sting of sticks
> and thorns and curses
> endured the constant bruise
> of burdens not their own
> the tendency of men to use
> and then discard rather than meet
> and pay the debt of gratitude.
> For them the future also held
> the knacker's rope, the flayer's blade
> the tearing of their bodies
> for the sparing of a race.
> In the shadows of that stable
> might it be his warmest welcome
> lay within their quiet comprehending gaze?

✿ ✿ ✿

And now what about those angels?
For they were certainly
a part of that whole scene.
Not just a part, indeed,
for as we read over once again
the Gospel treatments of Nativity
it becomes clear that they were in charge;
they positively directed–
stage-managed the entire enterprise
from start to finish.

It must have been
the busiest few months,
the most hectic, frantic time
the heavenly host had ever been through.
Not to get into that old business
of counting the number of angels
on the head of a pin,
yet I would be willing to wager
(if I did that sort of thing)
that there are more angels
per square inch of Scripture here
than anywhere before or since,
at least until the end of time
in the Book of Revelation.

What, then is their role?
What do these uncanny beings represent?
The word *angel* comes from a Greek word
angelos, meaning "messenger."
Take away the fancy trappings
that we find carved into the stone
of old cathedrals, melted through
the radiance of stained glass;
strip off the halos, shining robes,

the shimmering wings and harps
and what you have, in fact,
is a message bearer,
one who brings, who bears
the Word of God into the world.

They speak.
They speak today, if we will hear them.
The poet Francis Thompson wrote:

> The angels keep their ancient places;
> Turn but a stone, and start a wing!
> 'Tis ye, 'tis your estrangèd faces,
> That miss the many-splendoured thing.

But in order to hear we must remain open to
the true mysteries of life and death and love,
not run and hide deep in the forest of the facts.
These facts we make so much of
are simply fine, as far as they go,
simply fine for answering so many
of our practical, everyday questions.
But they are far too small, too narrow,
and too limited in their scope
alone to describe and deal with
the totality of what we all experience
as reality, as life within this
manifold and multi-faceted creation.

In that powerfully perceptive drama,
Saint Joan, by George Bernard Shaw,
the Dauphin questions Joan
in petulant anger about the voices
which she claims are guiding her.

> Oh, your voices, your voices. Why don't the
> voices come to me? I am king, not you.

Joan responds:

> They do come to you; but you do not hear
> them. You have not sat in the field in the
> evening listening for them. When the angelus
> rings you cross yourself and have done with
> it, but if you prayed from your heart and lis-
> tened to the thrilling of the bells in the air af-
> ter they stopped ringing, you would hear the
> voices as well as I do.

I am convinced,
as a result of hour upon hour of listening,
not just for God, but also to troubled individuals
within the quiet of my study walls,
we all can and do hear such voices,
voices that speak of a fairer, fuller world;
of a fellowship, not just of men and women,
black, white, and brown; rich and poor;
east, west and north and south;
but of all created being–
all that God has made–and that somehow,
someday yet, will praise him
through this babe that comes to Bethlehem.

We cannot understand them fully,
where they come from, how they reach us.
The very least that we can do is to wonder.
And that's what Christmas really is about–
wonder, in both senses of the word.
We can wonder and adore
at the marvel of the Savior's birth.
We can wonder and explore,
inquiring what this means,
what all of this implies for us,
just where we stand within the circle
of these faces at the manger,
within the vast, embracing circle

of the entirety of God's creation.
Because, as Saint Paul foresees the goal
and consummation of all things:
this entire universe itself
(from animals all the way through angels)
"is to be freed from the shackles of mortality
and enter upon the liberty and splendor
of the children of God."

The mystery, then,
and the manure of Christmas.
A cause for us to wonder, simply wonder.
And in this manufactured, matter-of-fact
twentieth century, that may not be
such a bad place to begin.

*"The Silent Seers" first appeared in *alive now!* (Nov./Dec. 1979).

Mary was not the only one with questions on her mind that first Christmas Eve. In the poem below I have portrayed a rather quizzical, even sceptical, time-and-work-hardened shepherd who is reflecting at some later date upon the events of that weird and mystical night.

THE SHEPHERD'S QUESTION

And this will be a sign for you: you will find a babe . . .

(Luke 2:12)

What kind of sign
was that, then?
Not the new star,
strange as that may seem;
not even the angels,
or those weird travelers from the east;
but a rag-wrapped baby in a feed box.
I ask you, was that a sign
to shake the gates of Hell,
or even Rome?

Yes,
there was blood around.
The signs of agony
still stained the wooden beams,
although the worst
had already been cleared away.
Birth
it was;
another birth.
No more–no less.

The baby nursed
like a whole world athirst–
power in those little jaws
seeking mother's milk
like love from heaven.
And that hand,
as firm upon the breast
as if he grasped the globe
of life itself and held it
strong and tender.

The sign
grew up,
or so I heard.
Came to a no-good end, they say.
Maybe that's all we can look for
from our signs–
a gleam of light,
a night of peace,
before they fade away.
Who knows?

The following meditation focuses on the response of the shepherds to the angels' song and all that followed.

THE SHEPHERDS AND THE ANGEL SONG

And in that region there were shepherds out in the field, keeping watch over their flock by night.
(Luke 2:8)

One of the things
that preachers tend to learn
too late in life
is how to ask the right questions
of this book of books, the Bible.

Go to the libraries,
scan the theological
and biblical bookshelves,
and you will find ream upon ream,
literally miles of tight-written pages,
filled with fascinating,
but ultimately quite marginal speculation
about the mights and maybes,
the perhapses and the possiblys,
that lie behind the stories in this old book.

We find, for example,
in the scripture commentaries,
the classic sermon collections,
that preachers in the past
have soared to great heights–
unfortunately also to great lengths–
rhapsodizing about the sheer simplicity

of these shepherds.
They point out how they represent
the common folk, the ordinary
person-in-the-street or on-the-hillside;
someone just like you or me.

Still others have theorized
that these men were actually outcasts,
disreputable rogues even, maybe, crooks;
those, at any rate, whose work conditions
made it impossible for them to keep up
with the requirements of the Jewish law;
and who therefore represented
at the cradle of our Lord,
the very sinners he had come to save.

A third school of thought
maintains that they were sacred shepherds,
chosen out for a particular task,
to be in charge of the select
and holy flocks of the Jerusalem temple.
This way such scholars discover
a symbolic linking in which
the newborn Lamb of God is greeted,
welcomed by the sacrificial lambs
of the old covenant.

Now these, one must agree,
are fascinating theories;
maybe even helpful, once in a distant while;
but they are fanciful, speculative at best,
and they fail to honestly address
the evidence set before us by the scriptures,
which is the only real evidence we have!

What, then, *do* we know about these shepherds?
If we cannot discover who they were,

or why they were out there
with their flocks
in the middle of the night–
when any sensible and responsible shepherd,
any keeper of the flock
who could tell the difference
between a crook and a fence post,
would surely have had his sheep
safely tucked into the fold–
one thing, at least, is clear:
we do know what they did.
And that, it seems to me,
is all we need to know;
is all that Luke–
who wrote the story in the first place–
is interested in having us know
about these Bethlehem shepherds.
We do know what they did.

I.

Those shepherds on the hillside
beheld the angel of the Lord
and they hearkened to his voice.

So what's so great about that?
That's hardly a major achievement,
particularly when you consider
that they had just been confronted by
quite some spectacular presentation.
If I ran into the heavenly host
singing out in the fields at midnight
I'd pay attention too!
Or would I?

An angel is simply a messenger,
a bearer of the Word of God;
and such messages, conceivably,

are coming to us all the time,
but we do not take the time,
or have the courage to listen.
In Truman Capote's *A Christmas Memory*,
Annie, the old spinster lady,
out flying kites one Christmas morn,
says to her youthful companion:

> I'll wager at the very end a body realizes the
> Lord has already shown Himself. That things
> as they are . . . just what they've always seen,
> was seeing Him.

God's word, then, comes to us
through "things as they are";
God's messengers, all those angels,
appear right at the heart of the everyday.
But unless we are listening,
unless we are prepared to drop, for a moment,
our busy work of preparation, celebration,
we will never hear the angels' song.

It's almost as if that angel
had already tried the innkeeper,
but he had no time even to hesitate;
already tried the soldiers
in the tavern down in Bethlehem,
but they were having too good a time;
and finally, as a last resort,
had come upon this pack of shepherds.
And these, at last, were folk who could hear–
could hear the best good news
this world has ever heard.
They were far enough "out of it,"
–don't you see?–far enough removed
from what today we insist on calling "reality"
–the fuss and bustle, jostle and hustle
of the marketplace–just far enough away

to enable them to hearken to eternity.

Nowadays it seems to be
an even harder task to listen,
what with the constant blasting
of the canned and souped-up carols;
the crass commercial hypes that seem
to occupy at least thirty of every sixty seconds,
the bleep and bloop of electronic gadgetry
sirening in our ears.
Yet despite all this,
there still is time to find
a quiet space to listen,
listen for the angels;
time even to begin with those about us,
those we love and live with,
by giving them the finest gift we can give,
the gift of our attention, our respect, our time,
the gift of our attentive, listening ear.
In that listening–who knows?–
we may even hear the angels' voices
singing "Peace on earth"
as those shepherds did so long ago.
For those shepherds listened.

II.

The second thing they did,
those quaking shepherds under the night sky,
is that they went . . .

> Let us now go even unto Bethlehem, and see
> this thing which is come to pass . . . and they
> came with haste and found Mary and Joseph,
> and the babe lying in a manger.
>
> (Luke 2:15-16, KJV)

I love that ancient wording from the King James
Version:

Let us now go even unto Bethlehem and see . . .

The more modern versions,
for the most part, fail miserably
to capture the mood of this dramatic scene.
"Let's go to Bethlehem," says one,
"and see this thing that has happened."
"Let's go . . ." Good grief!
You'd think they were proposing a midnight stroll!
There is an urgency here, a swift decisiveness;
yes, a sense of being caught up into
the midst of the momentous,
even a death-to-life quality
about this immediate decision
to seek out the newborn king.

Yet when one stops to think,
is it not all just a bit impulsive,
a bit hasty, even rash, this swift decision?
Should they not have gathered first
and formed themselves a committee,
a task force to investigate, elucidate,
evaluate this unprecedented incident,
then report back at the next
regular meeting of the shepherds' council?
Oh, I'm afraid, I get dreadfully afraid
that that is exactly how we,
how I, would respond . . .
through channels and
most decently and in order.

There are, of course,
times for channels; occasions
when it is vitally important to step back,
study, consider and reconsider,
debate and gather further information.
But there are also times

when procedures such as these
are a betrayal,
an act of craven cowardice.
In times like ours, for example,
when more people are going hungry,
more babies are starving, human bodies
and brains being crippled by malnourishment
than at any other time in history,
how much more information do we need,
how many more opinions must we hear,
before we act to stop this hunger holocaust?

Perhaps even more urgently,
in these days of global crisis,
when the social fabric of trust and cooperation
between nation and nation, tribe and tribe,
clan and clan appears to be not just fraying,
but actually ripping apart;
when the physical, chemical,
natural fabric which holds our globe
in delicate, miraculous balance
is also tearing at the seams
so that humankind itself may not
be coming to any new beginning,
as it did at that first Christmas,
but rather to an end, full stop;
are we doing anything about it?
Are we taking any hand in our own fate
and the fate of this whole earth;
or are we waiting until all the facts are in,
until, in other words, there will be
nothing left to do, except to pray?
The shepherds listened and then they acted.
They went, "even unto Bethlehem,"
and with haste to find
the Prince of Peace.

III.

The final thing
those shepherds did is,
I suspect, the most important of all;
for they returned:

> And the shepherds returned, glorifying and
> praising God for all the things that they had
> heard and seen.
>
> (Luke 2:20, KJV)

Shouldn't they have stayed?
Would it not have been better
if they had abandoned their sheep
and formed themselves into some kind of monastery,
praying, kneeling constantly beside the holy child,
observing, recording (maybe then we would have
known what Jesus did until the age of thirty),
worshiping each sacred moment
as he grew "in wisdom and in stature
and in favor with God and man" (Luke 2:52, KJV)?
Would not that have been a meaningful thing,
to have a lovely shrine, the sacred stable,
all preserved, and constantly adorned
by this faithful order of the shepherds?

But then what about the sheep—
those new pastures to be sought out,
spring's new crop of wool to be sheared
and hauled to market, the lambs
to be protected and provided for,
the constant injuries and ailments
that afflict even the best-kept flocks
to be tended, bound up, and made whole?
So the shepherds returned,
glorifying and praising God.

We have hearkened too.
We all have caught at least
a fragment of the angels' message.
And we have acted also–
have at least picked up this little book,
sat down a moment to be still,
reached in toward the soul.
We have torn ourselves away
from all the frantic busyness
of preparing to be happy
and made our own beginnings–
whatever they might be–
at that quite different task,
preparing for the Christ child.
And I dare say we will find him,
at least a momentary glimpse.
There are few of us whose hearts
will not be briefly touched,
whose eyes will not be momentarily dimmed,
one way or another over the next few days.

But what then?
What follows after Christmas?
Back to the flocks again,
to the old routines and daily desperations,
to managing somehow to stick it out,
survive, until next time
this season comes around and we can
once more be touched and moved
by mystery and wonder.
Is this, then, to be all there is–
an annual encounter, fleeting at the best,
with the very love of God incarnate?

IV.

It does not have to end that way.

It didn't for those shepherds.
They returned, yes, to their flocks,
but not the same, never again the same
as they had been before that holy night.
They returned, Luke tells us,
"Glorifying and praising God
for all that they had seen . . . ."

In my own vocation as a minister
over these holy Advent weeks,
the hurt of life does not become suspended,
magically put on hold
until the festive days are done.
I visit in the hospitals,
seek healing words of hope to speak
beside the beds of those who must face death;
try to hold out comfort, consolation,
to broken, grieving families;
or to nurture the frail spark of courage
in the hearts of individuals who have known
more than their share, perhaps,
of heartache and defeat.
Indeed the very setting of my work
amid all the Advent loveliness
of our sanctuary buildings
simply accentuates the irony,
points up the questions even more severely.
The festivity, you see, is not enough.
For all their beauty,
their genuine warmth,
the trappings and traditions of this season
cannot wipe out the bleak realities
that afflict people's lives.

But if we will look right to the heart—
beyond the holly wreaths and candles—
to a cold and bitter cowshed,

a hasty, unprovided, bloody birth;
if we can catch amid the bewilderment,
pain and fear, the clear confusion
of this refugee couple, Mary and Joseph;
if we can catch and hold a moment
the almost indescribable reality
of God, the Eternal One,
born in our midst to save us
as we are right here, right now,
yes, *in* all the ongoing pain,
bewilderment, and confusion
of our own lives;
then we have something to offer,
something that will last beyond the holidays,
beyond the taking down and storing
of the Christmas decorations.

We have a God whose cradle led him
to a cross and then to an empty,
shattered, finally defeated tomb.
We have a God whose love for us
will never let us go, will search us out,
come join us, walk with us
down all the daily paths of life
and even dusty death.
Here is the word of Christmas,
the strength in which we too–
just like the shepherds–
can return glorifying and praising God
for all that we have seen;
the faith and hope in which we can rejoice,
not only in this blessed season,
but on every blessed day of life from here
until the dawning of the kingdom.
> *Good Christian friends rejoice*
> *With heart and soul and voice;*
> *Now ye need not fear the grave:*

News, news, Jesus Christ was born to save!
Calls you one and calls you all
to gain his everlasting hall.
Christ was born to save,
Christ was born to save!

The role of Joseph in this entire Nativity sequence is an
ambivalent one. In what did his "fatherhood" consist? He had
to carry out all the traditional fatherly tasks and
responsibilities, yet without the privilege and delight of
actually fathering the child and proudly calling this child his
own. Is it too daring to suggest that he serve as stand-in for
God, the true Father of the babe, that night? Was Joseph foster
parent to the Almighty? What a delicate and complicated task
to find oneself destined to undertake!

JOSEPH:
FOSTER PARENT

Joseph, thou son of David, fear not.
(Matthew 1:20, KJV)

It always strikes me as ironic,
yet also strangely fitting,
that in the elegant line drawing of the Nativity
which graces the Christmas Eve bulletin cover
each year at my church–
as in so many such "manger scenes"–
there is no figure of Joseph to be seen.

Mary, of course, holds center stage,
and the blessed infant lies right there in her arms;
several farm animals may be discerned
in the shadows at the fringes;
there is even a suggestion of kings and shepherds,
but Joseph simply is not there.

I say this is strangely fitting because,
as I have discovered in reading and research

over the years, the role of Joseph–
Joseph of Nazareth, Joseph the Carpenter
Joseph the husband of Mary,
Joseph who stood at the manger–
the role of Joseph at the birth of the Messiah
seems to be an almost transparent one,
to be hardly there at all,
to be that of a virtual nonentity.

Oh yes, he did his bit beforehand,
in getting the pregnant mother
to that (soon to be illustrious) cowshed.
And later he will have his part to play again
as he leads the refugee Mary
and her newborn child in the flight to Egypt.
But at the birth itself,
those dramatic, moving scenes of nativity,
Joseph fades into the background
and well-nigh disappears.

Now Mary has her role;
that's clear and obvious enough.
She bears the child,
wraps him in swaddling cloths,
and lays him in the manger.
The shepherds also,
as we have already seen,
have their part to play
as they hearken to the angels
and come rushing from the fields–
telling all along the way
(I would assume, knowing how shepherds are)
of the stirring message they have heard.
And then, having seen the holy infant,
they go forth again, still glorifying
and praising their Lord God.

Those wise men from the east–
appearing on the scene a little later–
they too have lots to accomplish
as they bring their royal gifts,
present them to the child,
and work together to outwit
the wily plotting of King Herod.

But Joseph,
so far as we can tell
from the biblical record,
Joseph stands there,
simply stands there.

I remember being present
at the birth of Fiona,
our second daughter–
in those days
fathers were not allowed to be present
for the birth of a first child.
I confess I am a true type A,
my wife even calls me hyperactive!
One of the things I found most difficult
was to be unable to do anything at all–
no way to assist, pitch in,
organize an alternative approach!
All there was to do was stand there,
offering quiet comfort perhaps
–so long as I stayed out of the way–
be a witness at an event in which
I, myself, could play no part.

In Rembrandt's luminescent canvas,
The Adoration of the Shepherds,
we gaze into a medieval barn.
The scene is cast in shadows
and at deepest night,

but the firelight picks out for us
the kneeling shepherds there
before the crib,
their staffs in hand,
or laid aside on the rough floor.
One stands behind the rest,
an older figure holding a lantern.
A boy grasps tight the collar
of a large and evil-looking dog.
Mary cradles the infant with her arm,
looking peaceful, if somewhat pensive.
Two women chatter to each other
in the background,
while Joseph,
his hair tousled,
his face lined and worn with weariness,
stands, one shoulder thrust slightly forward
as if to protect her from the throng,
and gazes at the fire
with an anxious, worried look.

There must have been,
don't you see,
a kind of agony to being there,
a veritable torment to just standing there,
able to do nothing, say nothing that might help;
to stand and wonder what all this could mean
and fear at what might very well lie ahead
for his beloved Mary and this child
who was not even his . . .
to have to stand and simply be there.

Can we glimpse in this
a foretaste, a foreshadowing
in a lesser key, of the torment
of another Father who is compelled–
by His own plan and predestined design–

to stand by and watch as his own Son
bears willingly the burden of the cross,
faces down the very worst
that all the powers of evil
and of Hell can throw against him?

And the wonder of it,
the true miracle of Rembrandt's painting,
is that, if we are patient with it,
if we are prepared to give the time
to let the masterpiece speak to us,
we come to recognize that face;
we know the look of anguish Joseph bears
because we see it all too often
in this modern world of ours.

We see it on those faces
on the screen and in the newspapers
when tragedy and disaster has hit hard–
a fire, a flood, an earthquake,
an act of sheer insane brutality,
a so-called accident of war–
and there is nothing to be done.
Events have caught up human lives
just like a tide,
have swept them far beyond control,
then dashed them on the rocks.
And all that there is left to do
is be there, just be there.

It is a look
that I have had to see
too often in my daily pastor's rounds;
to see across the faces of a family
where death has entered in
and claimed and borne away a loved one
from the circle of their hearth.

It is a look of blank bewilderment
because we do not know how to react
when there is nothing, nothing at all,
that we can say or do to change things;
when everything we cherish is,
as they will tell us,
"in the hands of the Almighty."

Donald Wanderhope, the hero
(if we still have heroes nowadays)
of Peter De Vries' novel, *The Blood of the Lamb*,
the father of young Carol who is dying of leukemia,
finds himself inside a little Catholic church
close beside the city hospital.
He lights a candle
there at the shrine of Saint Jude—
patron saint of lost and hopeless causes—
then he prays:

> Give us a year. We will spend it as we have
> the last, missing nothing. We will mark the
> dance of every hour between the snowdrop
> and the snow: crocus to tulip to violet to iris to
> rose. We will note, not only the azalea's crim-
> son flowers. . . . We will seek out the leaves
> turning in the little-praised bushes and the
> unadvertised trees. . . . We will note the lost
> yellows in the tangles of that bush that spills
> over the Howards' stone wall. When winter
> comes, we will let no snow fall ignored. We
> will again watch the first blizzard from her
> window like figures locked snug in a glass
> paperweight. "Pick one out and follow it to
> the ground!" she will say again. We will feed
> the plain birds that stay to cheer us through
> the winter, and when spring returns we shall
> be the first out, to catch the snowdrop's first

white whisper in the wood. All this we ask,
with the remission of our sins, in Christ's
name. Amen.

The hardest task,
the most difficult role of all:
that of just being there.
And Joseph,
dearest Joseph stands for that.
Don't you see?

It is important,
crucially important,
that he stand there by that manger,
as he does,
in all his silent misery
of doubt, concern, and fear.
Because if Joseph were not there
there might be no place for us,
for those of us at least—
so many—who recognize and know
that heartache also for our own,
who share that helpless sense
of lostness, of impotence,
in our own lives, our families, our jobs,
in our fearful, threatened world this night.
Yes, in Joseph's look of anguish
we find our place;
we discover that we too
belong beside the manger:
this manger in which are met
God's peace and all our wars and fears.

There is something more
to be discovered in Rembrandt's painting,
something else we can find within
the role of Joseph, simply standing there,

silent, and so still.
There is, if we look carefully,
a light, a kind of radiance,
that shines upon his worried face,
a glimpse, a snatch at least–
beyond the weariness–
of something close to wonder.
There is a gradually dawning peace,
peace not just for sweet angelic cherubs
floating high on clouds above that stable–
Rembrandt doesn't even paint any of those–
but peace even for weary, worried,
fearful folk like Joseph;
folk like you, like me.

We seem to find so little peace
of any kind these days at Christmastime.
We get so occupied in doing things,
getting ready, making careful plans,
then bringing them to fruition.
It's the most hectic time of year,
after all, what with presents to be bought,
wrapped, and delivered;
cards to be mailed,
(even to those last-minute folk
you didn't expect to get one from this year–
and almost hoped you wouldn't–
given the price of stamps and all).
There are trees to be bought,
set up, and trimmed.
There are parties to be given,
to be gone to, and enjoyed–
and all of this to be accomplished
before a certain day, a certain hour,
or we will have missed our chance.
It will be too late; too late to give,
to welcome, or to greet until another year,

another Christmas rolls around–
as if it ever is too late for love!

Yet that's how we behave,
even if it's not how we believe.
And in this rush,
this festive Yuletide push and shove,
there's just no time for peace,
for standing still,
for simply *being there* in worry
or in wonder–or in both.

That stable too, in Bethlehem,
must have been a busy place on Christmas Eve,
what with birth and all its urgencies,
the visiting, worshiping shepherds
and the people they had told,
all crushing in to see.
Yet Joseph simply stands there.
"Don't just do something,"
is what he calls to us across the centuries,
into the midst of the hustle
and the bustle of this season,

> *Don't just do something,*
> *stand there.*

And so we come,
at last, into the stable;
a little breathless, to be sure,
a bit preoccupied, perhaps,
about those last few lingering items
still to be checked off before we close our eyes;
but we gather, just the same,
to rest our tired feet, to sing beloved songs,
to hearken to "sweet sounds
that give delight and harm not,"
ancient words that speak to us

of light in darkness,
hope beyond all fears.

Venite adoremus, says the carol.
"O come, let us adore him."
Not "let us serve him," you will notice;
nor, "let us work for, strive for,
live for, die for him."
All that may come in its own good time–
God's own good time.
But for this night at least,
this holiest of nights,
Venite adoremus.

Let us *be* there,
simply be there just as Joseph was,
with nothing we can do now,
nothing we can bring–
it's far too late for that–
nothing even to be said
except, "Behold–be blessed,
be silent, be at peace."

"Joseph, son of David,
do not fear," the angel said.
And Jim and Alice, Fred and Sue,
Bob and Tom and Jean and Betty, too,
the word to you, to all of us
here at the manger side,
the word is also, "do not fear."
Our God, the Lord and Sovereign,
Maker of heaven and earth,
time and eternity,
of life and death and all that is
and shall be,
has joined us in this moment,
shares our sorrow, knows our fears,

is well acquainted with our foolishness
and petty, selfish ways;
and still and all he brings us peace,
he bears us hope, he tells us,
"Just stop trying for one moment.
Just stop striving, stop all your doing
for this night of nights
and then believe and be, accept
and live, and know that you are mine
and you are blessed now and forevermore."

The hour is at hand.
The time is all fulfilled.
Venite adoremus.
If you miss him, then nothing else
in all this wide creation now
can take its place.
Venite adoremus.
The time is now–
that time when we must be there,
simply be there,
and adore.

This simple haiku breathes with the sigh of Joseph as he stands and witnesses the miracle of the mother and the child.

JOSEPH'S WISH

Rest, my Mary, rest.

Your child sleeps sound beside you,

All creation blessed.

*First appeared in *The Living Church*, December 23, 1990.

An imaginary character, this tough, case-hardened midwife speaks the poem below. Although she may never have stood beside the manger, the attitude she represents is one that greets the Christ-child wherever and whenever he is born into our midst.

THE MIDWIFE OF BETHLEHEM

Why do we make such a fuss,
after all, about birth?
Surely we know what is happening,
bound to happen sooner or later–
disease, drink, cold blind accident,
too little food, too many brains,
the usual and always final event
gets them all, get us all in the end.
So why, in the name of heaven,
are all these idiot shepherds here,
far from their fold, fouling the air
and the streets with their rancid flocks?
And these dark, distinguished strangers,
confused, spent with much travel,
mumbling together of stars, gold, other gifts?
Indeed you'd think even the dumb beasts
in their stalls had been told something
and were waiting, reverent somehow
at this hasty, unprovided birth.
Yet, when all is said and done,
there was something about that young mother,
trusting, calm, confident for a first timer.
And the baby, so bold, aware already. . . .
Why, I do believe the child is smiling,
looking right over here, bless my soul, at me.

Get out of my way, sheep,
while I kneel a moment, rest my weary legs
before I leave, and view this newest infant
that my red old hand has slapped
from death to free and gasping life
this odd, and almost holy night.

*Reprinted from *Weavings: A Journal of the Christian Spiritual Life* (November/December, 1991), Vol. 6, No. 6. Copyright 1991 by The Upper Room. Used by permission.

*While he is never mentioned in the scriptures, there must
certainly have been an innkeeper, someone to tell the travel-
worn couple that there was "No room at the inn." Various
writers and traditions have portrayed this person, some more
sympathetically than others. My presentation shows an eager
entrepreneur, anxious to assure all and sundry that whatever
happened that night was not his fault and should not be
allowed to reflect discredit upon his worthy establishment.*

THE INNKEEPER'S DEFENSE

Of course there was room.
Any innkeeper worthy of his bread
and salt knows that.
Even in the most travel-wearied vacation season,
always, within reason, one chamber,
at the least, is kept
for that noble, but unexpected guest,
that personage of means and influence,
accustomed to the very best accommodation,
who arrives without reservations
and tests to make or break
your reputation as a host.

Yes, there was room.
But who, for God's sake,
was going to take in a female
in her all-too-typical condition?
So far along she might well have the thing
that very night . . . and then what of my fine furnishings
and white imported linen sheets?
To say nothing of the fright her peasant shrieks
and groans would wreak upon the tender ears

of all my cultivated customers,
sending them to an early bed,
or driving them from the place disgusted,
maybe never to return.
To add to all of this,
there was the matter of liability.
After all, I carry no coverage
for such eventualities beneath my humble,
if otherwise well-protected roof.

Pretty bit she was though,
for a country lass.
In other circumstances
she might well have shared my room,
and even more. . . .
The husband seemed a dour and dogged type.
These yokels can be dangerous, you realize;
best keep your distance,
have no dealings with them.
Anyway, I sent them along
to the lower quarter of town.
Plenty midwives down there
to make things easier with their hot water,
implements, and swaddling stuff.
One a year, you know, these people have—
son or daughter—
and all the shapes and colors under heaven.
She would be happier among
her own rough kind.

But I want you to remember this.
There *was* room. Not a doubt.
I wouldn't want any other impression to get about.
I keep a most commodious establishment
where no one with the wherewithal,
or recognized connections,
need ever fear that they might be shut out

without a place to lay their head.
Foxes have holes, they say,
and the birds of the air have nests,
and the innkeeper of Bethlehem
will always have a resting place
for distinguished members of the human race.

II

KINGS

Awakening from a nightmare, perhaps provoked by his
uncanny visitors from the East, this clever, cruel plotter of a
monarch responds with that swift decisiveness that has
brought him to such a post of power and privilege.

HEROD DREAMS

Fish, there were,
great schooling shoals,
and one who strolled among their ripples
tall as a shepherd with his flocks.

Temple jars
tipped over scattered tables,
trickled blood,
or was it wine?
across a mellow face
that laughed so long and fine
he washed the slopes of Olive Mountain
with his tears.

There limped a donkey
ringed with dusty cheers
beneath a harlequin
who palmed my fearful city as his own.
While at his broken heels
vast festal meals were spread
for royal guests and vagabonds
all supping simple bread with ruby vintage.

Drunken star songs
rolled along bright heavens
to a stable brimmed

with sheepfold men and magi.
Those murmuring strangers,
once again,
casting their purple
calculations on the night.

I thought I saw a gallows cross
become a throne, high, lifted up
through rending grave clothes
and a splintered stone.
Then, as it ended,
a whole regiment of children,
infants really, danced me from my palace
piping through the gaping lips of bloody Sheol.

This dream
demands
immediate interpretation.
Send for my guards!

While they belong in almost every manger scene, the three kings, according to the Gospel narratives, came on the scene a little later. This meditation and series of poems explores their presence and participation in this holiest of events.

INTRODUCING THE MAGI

Now when Jesus was born in Bethlehem of Judea in the days of Herod the king, behold, there came wise men from the east to Jerusalem, saying, Where is he that is born King of the Jews?
(Matthew 2:1-2, KJV)

Matthew never calls them kings;
that idea seems to have crept in later
from the prophecies in Isaiah and the like.
As far as this Gospel is concerned
these individuals were magi,
wise men, probably astrologers,
given their familiarity with the stars.

Their role is an intriguing one,
far fuller and richer
than that of the shepherds,
bringing on the scene, as they do,
the first looming intimations
of another power than that
which came to earth at Bethlehem.
The wily wickedness of Herod
outwitted by the warning to the magi
and their own sagacious cleverness
foreshadows from the start
the evil forces which will threaten
this child's life,

and their eventual defeat.

These mysterious sages
(even their number–three–
has to be inferred from the symbolic gifts)
and their long journey
in search of the messiah
have captured the imagination
of people–seekers and believers,
poets, preachers too, ever since that time.
Of all the faces at the manger,
these are the ones most alien
and strange, most difficult to comprehend,
to identify with and feel at home with.
Yet that very strangeness
has tantalized the storytellers
and mythmakers; not to mention
the minds of little children.

I love the story of the boy
attending his first ever Christmas pageant
who glanced behind him in the darkness
and caught sight of the three kings
entering the sanctuary from the rear.
"Don't look now" he whispered
to his mother, "but God just got here . . .
only I'm not sure which one he is."

They are generally portrayed
as elderly, with beards–
wise men always used to be old.
Traditionally their names
are Caspar (no, not the friendly ghost),
Melchior, and Balthazar;
and one of them is black.
Garrison Keillor,
of Lake Woebegon fame,

still maintains that,
since they represent the Gentiles,
one of them must have been Lutheran
(bearing–naturally–a plate
of tuna noodle hot dish)!

In the poems that follow
I have tried to capture something
of the different personalities
and mindsets represented
by these characters.
They all seem somewhat puzzled–
as I feel sure these characters were;
the wisdom of this world,
as Paul reminds us,
makes very little sense of the ways
and wondrous workings of God's grace.
At times a note of weary,
dare one say, wistful cynicism
may be heard, but Christmas
wouldn't be Christmas without that note,
even though the song of the angels
almost manages to drown it out.

I hope my kings and wise men
speak, not only to the cynic
and the disillusioned within all of us,
but also to the song that yearns
to find its voice in each
and every one.

These magi find their wisdom redirected from the foretelling
of the future to the unveiling of the significance of the present
moment in all its givenness.

DISCOVERING THE PRESENT

Our trade is with the future,
as a rule,
charting the bright courses, channels,
navigations of the distant lighted vessels
of the heavens, probing through the viscera
of sacrificial beasts,
observing birds in flight, relating
visions of the night to what will come
to pass in days and years ahead.

This white and mobile star, however,
tells us nothing of what is to be,
directs the sight instead
toward what is.
I mean the present, here and now,
and what, or better, *who* is born
within this tight yet waking moment.
The Presence of new life
awaits our presence
and the precious gifts we too might bear
inside the stable of the self.

The following portrayal of one of the wise men draws freely–I must confess–on a type of learned present-day academic whose sophistication and self-satisfaction with his own "wisdom" blinds the eyes to any genuine discovery, to any kind of honest revelation.

WISE MAN

As a field trip it was,
let me say, reasonably productive.
Although, when you consider the expenses we ran,
and the time span involved,
it certainly could have been more profitable.
It must be emphasized
that the subsequent development
of my own professional reputation
owed nothing whatsoever to the episode.
The reports of our findings never did receive
the scholarly attention that they merited;
never even published,
if my memory still serves correctly–
lying on a library shelf somewhere
gathering dust.

The child seemed quite unexceptional,
despite the rather bizarre surroundings.
We presented–I clearly remember this–
the symbolic gifts: frankincense, myrrh,
even a little gold, just as called for
in the original proposal.
But the response of the parents
was disappointing, to say the least.
Ignorant peasants, nothing more.

And they seemed genuinely puzzled
by all the attention they were receiving.
A little scared too, I recall–
yes, quite terrified really,
now that I think of it–
especially the mother.

My colleagues–an odd pair themselves,
to tell the truth–seemed to concur
with my overall impressions.
And yet there was a certain naïve appeal
about the entire incident, a rustic simplicity
that might have been quite touching,
perhaps, in other circumstances.
We stayed an hour; but seeing scant opportunity
for further basic research, and feeling,
it must be admitted, somewhat homesick
for the conveniences of civilization,
we departed, taking care to return by
an even more circuituous route in order to preserve
this minor, yet fascinating specimen profile
of the birth of a cult-myth for later researchers.

Unfortunately, to this date,
there have been none.

This wise man begins in a similar vein to the one on the previous page, reminiscing in a detached and rather clinical way about the experience they had undergone some years before. But in stanza two he is caught up in the ever present miracle of the incarnation of Immanuel—God with us.

GIFTS GIVEN AND RECEIVED

We arrived on the scene weary
and too late for the actual birth;
but from all reports it would seem to have been
a normal procedure: no visions, visitants, portents,
unless, of course, you consider the star
that led us all that dreadful way
(a matter of celestial science, actually,
hardly a sign available to the public at large).
Oh yes, there were local peasants
who claimed to have seen a whole skyful of angels
but had only their sheep for witnesses;
that, and a look of late and joyous dignity.
We had brought gifts,
unusual items to be sure,
but proper in this case, knowing what we do today
about the fate of the recipient.

I speak of the infant thus
because I have no other words
with which to name the child we saw
and recognized, and failed to recognize.
The thing is, you see,
I felt throughout a sense that all our journey
was nothing at all, a single step
in comparison to the distance

and the proximity we met within that broken manger.
Near and far ceased to exist.
Everything and everywhere was present;
present also in the sense of given,
gifted once, for all, forever.
We had not come to him,
but he to us, and the birth
that, as I said before, we really missed,
took place anyway in us, in everything that night;
takes place again right now as I recall the way it was
to give a gift and then receive
this present in return.

Once again, in a slightly different voice, this wise man tells of the contrast between the very ordinary surroundings and the most extraordinary effect of the birth that took place in those surroundings.

EPIPHANY?

This star discloses nothing
that we have not seen before.
A cattle-cave with straw, the stolid beasts,
a couple caught in poverty and cruel circumstance,
and a child, newborn, with all the customary
trappings of exhaustion followed by relief,
blood, bandages, and that strangely childlike
look of first-time parents.
What was it, then, that set
this towering within, that moved us,
as if gazing from some sudden, dizzy height,
to gasp with wonder even as
we grasp for something to hold onto?
Is every birth attended in this way?
Does such a leap lie just beneath the surface
of all things and every moment? And, if so,
should we have jumped, and
can we still?

This contemporary king is one I encountered one recent Christmas Eve processing down the aisle of our church with a most embarrassed air as the organ played "We Three Kings of Orient Are." I hope that my imagination caught an accurate glimpse of what was going on behind that false beard, beneath that pasteboard crown.

THE KING IN SPITE OF HIMSELF

So what, in the name . . .
am I doing here
decked out
in tinsel crown and trailing
royal velvet gown behind
to pace with steep, majestic frown
this pew-lined aisle
just like a bride floats down
serene to greet her groom?

She got me into it, my bride—
I mean, said it was the least
I could do, and besides the kids
would thrill to see their dad in church
on Christmas Eve. No, I'm not a member,
one per couple was enough to get them
baptized. She joined, of course,
even teaches church school, which is
how, I guess, this all began.

Anyway, here I stand before the steps,
stage, manger, and that blue-caped Mary.
Next I must enter, kneel, present this gold
foil-wrapped cigar box. What a farce . . . a fake!

Sure be glad to make it home again
with a stiff drink or two. Funny,
how I'm shaking . . . you'd never think
the music got to you like this,
faces of the kids, eyes deep with wonder.

Wonder if that baby in the straw there
really sees me,
if it's me she's smiling to. . . .
These tears–for God's sake–
smear my make-up, take me,
as I struggle to my knees,
far back across the years
to wonders long forgot, found new again
this eve of sudden holy wonder.

III

CHRISTMAS
MEMORIES

Many families arrange their own "faces at the manger" each year as they place the varied pieces of their treasured Nativity scenes somewhere at the center of their homes. Such pieces often have a story attached that goes beyond the original Christmas story and carries its meaning into the present day.

TERRA COTTA CRÈCHE

We bought the set at Chartres
twenty years ago and more in the
frugal, fledgling years of early marriage—
discovered it in the cathedral shop,
new descended from the terrifying climb
up to the tower, all those catwalks sheer
along the awful edges. Then the little nun
who watched us, gentle, as we counted francs,
then counted them again.
We left the place without it,
splurged instead on *jus de fruit*
at a jukebox-sounding sidewalk table,
reasoned one more time over needs and necessaries.
How she rushed to find wood shavings and a box
to hold those terra-cotta figurines, almost as if
she knew that, twenty years and more from then,
our Christmases would blossom still with
radiance of Chartres, windows, wonder!

The eternal child, who still lives–so long as there is Christmas–within each and every one of us, is the focus of the meditation which follows.

ETERNAL CHILD

I.

No, not the babe himself–
there's been, perhaps, enough and more,
written about that sacred infant
in story, song, and verse.
The child I mean is one whose name
is every name, whose face is seen within
the faces of all children everywhere,
whose eyes shine with the light of each
and every child who ever lived,
who ever hoped for such a day,
for such a gift of love as Christmas
has become for children
all across this globe.

There *must* have been a child
somewhere in that stable,
gathered with the rest about that manger.
Even setting sentiment aside–
a dangerous thing to do at any time
and especially at Christmas–
the witness of tradition
combined with all that Jesus taught us
about the essential role of childhood
in the faith he came to share,
all this supports my own persuasion
that at least one child was to be found
around the cradle where the mother

laid her newborn child,
our Savior.

It might have been
one of the shepherd's youngsters:
Menotti's magic story of *Amahl* has set
to words and music that entrancing possibility.
Or could the innkeeper have had a daughter,
sent by her dad to lead the weary couple
to their place of shelter,
help them make the most of such refuge
as could be provided at such a time
and in such hectic circumstances?
One of the children from the town,
an urchin from the streets, perhaps,
would certainly also be a likely candidate.
Whatever . . . there must have been a child there.

II.

Part of the truest joy of Christmas
is remembering what it felt like as a child;
the keen and mounting anticipation,
secrets among family and friends,
fantastic tales of Santa and his elves,
songs and special programs in the schools,
daily delights of cards and parcels
in the mail, and the hope, this year,
for falling, drifting snow on Christmas Eve.

We had an artificial tree
we kept all through the war years–
minus an odd limb or two–
with a battered golden tinsel star
which grew more tilted and more tarnished
each time we took it from its box.
The decorations–including a toy trumpet
you could actually toot upon–

diminished also as the years went by
so that, by the time old Hitler's goose
was cooked, our tree was pretty bare.

I remember . . . I remember . . .
I don't suppose I'll ever forget
that Christmas morning when Mum and Dad,
in an inspired moment, had pegged
our stockings to the banister
with clothes pins so that,
as we crept down the darkened stairs
in pre-dawn shadows toward the tree,
our fingers stumbled across sheer delight
before we even had the time to waken properly.

It seems odd now
but the actual gifts,
those splendors we looked forward to
so eagerly, have vanished, for the most part,
from my memory without a trace.
I do recall a crenelated fort
one year whose sturdy cardboard walls
protected, in their turn,
both King Arthur's armored knights
and Beau Geste's Foreign Legion.
A picture-book version of Pinocchio
became the cause for bitter tears
when my infant brother used it
to try out a whole new set of crayons.
And many a cold winter's night
was cuddled into warmth around a small,
teddy-bear shaped, hot water bottle
which arrived beneath the tree
one Christmas morning.
These, along with the usual
and dull-but-useful items
from the never-idle fingers

of innumerable industrious aunts—
pairs of knitted gloves and socks
and scratchy woolen balaclava helmets
for those frigid wartime winters—
are all that linger now of the things
that I looked forward to.

III.

Looking back
with the perspective of the years,
one comes to realize that, even as a child,
the gifts were not what made this season
warm and wonderfully bright.
The moments, moods, sensations
are what live still in the memory,
are what radiate even all the way
to this present season now in preparation
and bring to it the savor
and the fragrance of enchantment;
the people, stories, songs,
customs, and old family traditions;
above all else a feeling of being home
at last, of finally discovering
that unique place and time and setting
one had searched for from the very start,
from a time before one even knew
what searching really meant.

It is an atmosphere of welcoming
and belonging, a presence of vast kindness
which is endlessly forgiving,
an assurance that everything needed
has already been provided and much more,
all this presided over by an all-pervasive
spirit of generosity and grace,
of delight in making happy,
of fulfilment in the filling up

and brimming over of every hollow cup,
of completion in the glad reunion
and rejoining of each and every broken,
severed, separated entity of life.

And this,
this legacy of hope
and trust and promise
for the future, somehow,
someday, comes to us with a child,
comes to us as a child, as we are led
into the paths of Christmas yet to come.
That is why no Christmas yet
has ever quite lived up to expectation.
But it will. In God's good time
and in the smiling promise of the child,
it will.
The child that is within me
and still waits beside that manger
knows that it will.

More memories, these of Anglo-Scottish Christmas seasons,
form the basis for another look at the eternal child and that
other child who was and is and ever shall be the Eternal One.

BOXING DAY DELIGHT

Boxing Day is what we called it
back in England, day after Christmas Day
when all those who delivered to the door–
the tradesmen, clattering milkman, postman,
paperboy, grocer's boy, driver of the baker's
van which smelled so heavenly steaming rich of
hot new bread, fresh scones and teacakes mixed with
all the warm and tangy odors of the patient steady
horse harnessed in front and munching on its nose bag;
there was the butcher's boy on a bicycle, his apron
blue and white and flecked with spots of blood,
bearing along a whiff of the sawdust floor,
the hanging sides of beef and pork,
the suet and the sausages as he delivered cool,
yielding brown-wrapped parcels at the kitchen door–
all these received their Christmas Box, which
must in Dickens' time have been a veritable box,
a carton filled with "Xmas Cheer" of sundry sorts.
But, by my early youth, this all had settled for
a sixpence or a shilling,
or if you were really lucky, maybe half-a-crown.
Whatever, it spread the generous
season out for us another day, postponed that dreary
moment when you fall back into winter wondering if
you will ever make it through till spring.

Another favorite for Boxing Day

was to attend the pantomime, or "Panto"
as it everywhere was known.
Boxing Day was always best for that,
although the show
continued on till well after
the holidays had ended.
They would take a fairy tale or nursery rhyme,
" Puss in Boots," "Old Mother Hubbard,"
"Dick Whittington" I liked best,
and flesh it out into a full-length show
with folk dressed up as animals,
men playing crotchety old dames,
young buxom women cast as handsome lads
and lots of slapping feathered hats on flashing thighs;
and music, trapdoors, vulgar jokes, and pratfalls,
sometimes even fairies flying out across the audience
of which the first five rows formed
"The Enchanted Forest,"
flying on thin invisible wires
you could almost hardly see
if you half closed your eyes.
Well, such a day!

I wonder nowadays just what the Christ Child
would have made of Boxing Day back then.
Would he pour scorn and judgment
over all those patronizing little gifts,
symbols of an unequal social order?
Might he denounce the commonness,
the tawdry tinsel glitter of the Panto
and its creaking old performers?
But then, again,
perhaps the Child would laugh and cry and cheer
and clap his hot and sticky hands with glee
just like we did as the evil-hearted
villains were defeated,
maidens saved, and heroes at last vindicated.

Might he even clasp a sixpence to himself
and run back home to share it,
conscious only of the gift which made
at least one further day shine bright
with heaven's brimming generosity?

T
R
I
M
TRIMMING
M
I
N
G

We
did
the tree
again tonight
–family style–
with all the usual
traditional disputes
about which box to open
first, who gets to hang what,
precisely where to set the Shains'
glass bird which has survived (Praise God!)
seven such arguments already.
The lower branches were,
as is the custom, heavy laden,
three or four gems per stem while only
a few furtive adult transfers rescued the
last two feet from stark and lonely nudity.
The lamps flickered a moment
and went out necessitating testing
each and every tiny oriental bulb
(or were they Italian?)
at least three times. The flasher either
didn't work or worked too well till somehow
it relented and the show was on.
Turn
out
the
light
a truce to every running
fight, come see what is
reflected for one instant
in tomorrow's wide
dark eyes!

IV

CHRISTMAS
MOMENTS

*Now and then, the face within the manger sneaks up on you,
catches you unawares within–for this example–in a dearly
loved, familiar countenance. And then, behold! you are in the
presence of incarnation.*

ADVENT SATURDAY MORNING WITH CATRIONA IN NEW YORK

Hanging on beside you as the crosstown bus
lurches its laden way between the wintered hills
of Central Park, my sidelong glance snags
on a prospect never caught before,
glimpsing within your early teenage profile
the full maturity of middle age, the aspect you
will one day wear as mother, one who bears
the future on firm shoulders.
But see now, what the eyes betray in that
slightest hint of drawing down toward the edge,
as though a weariness lies buried,
waiting to be born. My own well-worn
paternal eyes seek momentary refuge;
only to be captured, upon opening,
by the clear, unclouded sunrise of your smile.
Thanking the great Provider of such moments over
thirteen years of grace, I leave the crowded bus,
lead you dashing across Madison into elegant
Saint James' to meet, under the Advent wreath,
a harpsichord and string ensemble, rehearsing
with the soloists tomorrow's version of *Messiah*.
> *Behold, a virgin shall conceive,
> and bear a Son,
> and shall call his name
> Emmanuel, God with us.*

And through a sudden storm of tears
I grasp the wounding, mending holly branch,
claiming the spiral mystery of word made flesh
and secret lodged within the solemn
turning of the years.

The Coming of the Light

*My congregation maintains the lovely custom, as do many
others, of reenacting the coming of the light. We do this at the
close of the midnight service to herald the arrival of
Christmas Day. Each worshiper receives a small candle as
they enter the church. At the stroke of twelve the sanctuary is
darkened and two acolytes light their tapers from the chancel
candlesticks, the only lights left burning. Then they move
through the church in silence lighting the candelabra, the tall
aisle candles and one small, hand-held candle at the
beginning of each pew. The light is passed from hand to hand
along the pews until the entire vast room is radiant with the
golden, mellow light of six hundred candles; and we all sing
"Silent Night." It is a quietly powerful experience; but most
of the congregation, because of their seating, miss one of the
loveliest aspects. Seated in the chancel, I am privileged to
watch as the darkness is gradually illumined by row after row
of golden, haloed faces; faces, many of them, I have come to
know and care for through times of stress or great happiness
in the year drawing to a close. It is a magical moment, one for
which I am most grateful. The two poems that follow attempt
to share something of that Christmas morning vision.*

The Coming of the Light

A
pure
and
golden
light it
seems that
spreads across
the pews reflects
its radiance from the
mellow old carved oak
and hanging greens upon
the faces, hands of those
who sing so sweetly
"Silent Night." Look deep
into this gentle fire
and then go forth to bear
it far and tender to
wherever infants cold
and frightened tremble
in the dark with
no bright star
no kings
to
greet

LIGHT BEARERS:
CHRISTMAS EVE AT MIDNIGHT

Do
they
perceive
what they
are doing
while they
carry fire
from pew
to

darkened pew, first
kindling tall tapers
on the aisle, stoop-
ing then to a tiny
hand-held candle whose
flame is trembling,
passed along the row?
Will they pause to
see the way that light
progresses front to rear
a waxing golden bright-
ness that illumines
faces, lips that move
in "Silent Night"?
Or are they caught up in
tradition of their own,
a liturgy passed down
from youth to youth
makes them so anxious to
coordinate with partner's
steps deliberate across
the aisle, seeking the
small miracle of perfect
timing and thus missing
the perfection now
revealed behind their
measured footsteps as
radiance proceeds from
source to goal and
darkness yields to
newborn, fragile,
fondly sheltered light?

Those faces at the manger long ago, as we have seen, become all mixed in with, and then, perhaps miraculously, transformed into the multitude of faces that surround us, sing to us, appeal to our generosity or guilt, smile upon us and, at times, threaten to engulf us. The poem which follows seeks to sum up all the confusion of hopes, dreams, possibilities, and impossibilities that assail us in this season and summon them to kneel beside the crib.

I'M DREAMING

I'm dreaming
of a right Christmas
when every item that I buy
will be on sale and also
the ideal gift for persons
who have everything already.
I'm dreaming of a bright Christmas
when the tree lights work first time
and flash their brilliant message of success
from every tasteful, decorated, artificial,
non-allergenic yet natural lookalike limb.
I'm dreaming of a lite Christmas when,
no matter how much fruit cake, cookies,
eggnog, champagne, other goodies I consume,
my weight will magically fall to just below the average.
I'm dreaming of a write Christmas when all my cards
bear personal, intimately joyful greetings
and arrange themselves in matching multitudes
on every horizontal dust-free surface.
I'm dreaming, but I'll bet that what I get
will be the usual trite Christmas,
impolite Christmas, damp-with-fog-not-white

Christmas,
tight Christmas, goodnight Christmas,
bank-will-not-underwrite Christmas.
I'm praying that, despite Christmas,
I find myself midnight Christmas
able to invite Christmas and its newborn child
to stay and light a way into my Christmas-darkened
heart.

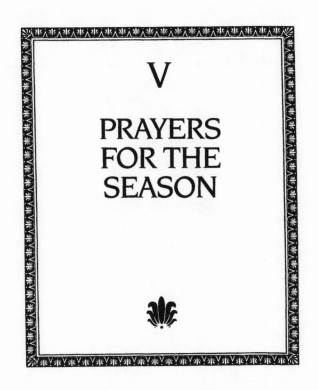

V

PRAYERS
FOR THE
SEASON

Four prayers for the season bring this book to a close. Yet everything within these pages is written in the spirit of prayer. My prayer is that those who pray these pages may go on to live them in the days and months ahead.

A PRAYER FOR LIGHTING ADVENT CANDLES

Father, this is a lovely thing we do,
to light more candles week by week
until your Son is born among us.
As the light of these candles grows,
so let the love of Christmas,
the joy of giving,
the happiness of hoping,
spread through our homes, our families,
our churches, our own lives,
that we might come at last
to kneel before the manger
and know the child of Christmas born
within our hearts.
Amen.

A Prayer for the First Sunday in Advent

Once again in this holy season, O God,
we listen to words of promise spoken by Isaiah
long ago:

> Every valley shall be exalted . . .
> and the crooked places made straight.

Lord, even in the high and holy days that lie ahead
there will be valleys, quiet moments of aloneness,
of desolation, of remembering loved ones absent,
family members perhaps long gone,
hopes that were never quite fulfilled,
plans and promises long shattered.

And there will be the crooked places also,
when the worst that is in us springs to life again,
the heart twists, the mind turns in upon itself,
and we know jealousy and malice, anger or greed.
For even in these highest days
we are still ourselves,
your dreaming, hoping children
who can yet stumble and fall,
go far astray along the way.

Make our crooked places straight
by your power, not our own.
Exalt the valleys of our lostness

and loneliness with your love.
And when the feast is over,
the last gift opened,
the final carol sung,
stay with us and stay for us
and hold us in your newborn
yet eternal arms forever.
Amen.

AN ADVENT SEASON PRAYER

This Advent season is so full
so crammed with human emotions—
the wondering anticipation of little children,
the joy and anxiety of parents,
the grinding loneliness of those far from
family and home,
the glimmering hope of all who find
the meaning of their life laid in a humble manger,
the weariness and despair of those
who cannot believe the old, old story
and thus see only the false
and ugly aspects of our celebration.

Break in—
break in to all our lives this day, Lord Jesus.
Come to us as you came long ago,
in gentleness and tender vulnerability.
Evoke in all of us
that love which alone can save us,
and through us save your world.

In this season of giving and receiving,
we pause a moment to recall the gifts
you bless us with at Christmas.

We thank you for your snow,
coming down like a quilt upon our busy world
and quieting us, slowing us down,

compelling us–willy-nilly–
to take time to be with ourselves.

For your stars, we bless your name,
frosted so bright by these December nights,
lifting up our eyes, raising our heads,
signaling across the centuries,
the vastness, the infinity,
the sheer and splendid glory
of your creation.

For your birds, we are grateful,
companying with us through the winter,
brightening the grays and whites
of our landscape with flashing reds
and blues, rich browns and blacks,
reminding us of springtime,
of birdsong, of nesting,
and of summer suns.

For your trees and bushes
we return our thanks;
for the fragrant, lively evergreens–
balsam and fir, spruce, hemlock, pine,
and bitter, red, and glossy holly;
primeval trees that know the depth of winter,
have learned to live with grace amid the cold.

For children, O God, we bless you;
young lives that call us back into our truest selves,
blessing us with their wonder,
their games and songs, their curiosity,
their needs so simply satisfied after all–
a candy cane, a coloring book, a kiss.

And for the child of Bethlehem,
your Word made flesh, your love alive

and mangered with us,
rejoicing in our waiting hearts this holy season
through each and every one of these
your gifts.

For all these gifts we bring our thanks,
and add a prayer for those whose blessings
have been hard to find, whose joys
tend to be few and far between,
asking that somehow we might be a blessing to them
in the name and for the joy of the babe in the manger.
Amen.

A Post-Christmas Prayer

Our Advent season is now ended
for another year.
All our waiting, those long days of anticipation,
have been fulfilled on Christmas Day
with the birth of your son, our Savior.
We thank you for all the joy we have known
and shared in this holy season.
We thank you that, as we have opened our hearts
to your presence, so you have come in,
been born anew into our days.

Yet, in this season
of fulfillment and genuine joy,
we must remember those whose joy is
still to be fulfilled,
all those whose Advent time of expectation
did not come to an end,
all who still await your coming
even though our Christmas is now ended.

We remember too
all held hostage in this season
by any kind of bondage whatsoever.
We pray for prisoners and their families;
we ask your strength for alcoholics and other addicts
and for their families also.
Lord, break all the bonds that hold your people captive,
and set us free for the life you have given us

in Christ our Lord.

We think of those among us,
within our circle of friends,
who still wait for your coming as
the deliverer from pain or grief or loneliness;
your coming to their empty, dreary, meaningless lives
with hope and purpose, even a glimpse of glory.

There are those whose needs
are yet more obvious;
who, despite all our Christmas generosity,
still look for your coming to them
in the simplest forms of bread to eat
and shelter from the cold.
For all refugees across the world tonight
we seek your presence and your comfort.

And last, O God, for ourselves,
those who, even in the midst of gaiety
and fun and gifts galore, know a hunger
that is not yet satisfied.
Help us in the year that lies ahead
to gain a new perspective on our days,
that we might seek, with your aid,
the truer, lasting things of life;
that we might learn to grow, as Jesus did,
"in wisdom and in stature
and in favor with God and man . . ."
Thus may the year that lies ahead
be a year of true renewal
through the Lord of life-renewed,
our Savior, Jesus the Christ.
Amen.

Printed in the United States
22878LVS00006B/469-498